To Brin
with love
Sally

Lady (Patsie) Fisher, great niece
of the famous Isabella Beeton,
lived in County Down and founded
the Women Caring Trust in 1972.

*All profits from the sale of this book go to
the Women Caring Trust, a non-sectarian,
non-political charity which helps children
in Northern Ireland.*

First published in Great Britain in 1998 by
Bellew Publishing Company Limited
8 Balham Hill, London SW12 9EA

© Sally Grylls 1998

ISBN 1 85725 129 6

Typesetting by Anthony Nelthorpe

I Remember It Well....

My Mother, Patsie Fisher, was painting the kitchen in our home in Northern Ireland when over the radio came an announcement that women who cared were gathering from all over the Province to join a peace movement in Belfast.

She rushed off, and returned home that evening determined to do something positive herself to help. That day laid the foundation for the formation of "Women Caring Trust" which has helped so many women and children in need during these troubled years.

My mother was Mrs Beeton's great niece. Like her great aunt she was a gifted hostess, a natural cook and "Household Management" was her bible!

Just before Patsie's sudden and unexpected death she discussed with me the idea of compiling a recipe book to commemorate 25 years of "Women Caring Trust". She felt that the format should be healthy recipes, which the children as well as the grown-ups would appreciate. So with the help of Ethel Bell, who worked with my mother to create and cook the wonderful treats which we as children enjoyed with our friends, I have compiled a few of our family favourites.

I think Patsie would approve of the ones we have chosen. I know she would be pleased that her idea has become a reality, and I hope everyone who buys this book will enjoy it.

Sally Grylls

1

Patsie on her favourite rock near Donaghadee with 'Smiles' named after her great grandfather, Samuel Smiles – author of '*Self-Help*'. Samuel Smiles was married to Isabella Beeton's half-sister, Lucy Dorling. Their son William, was a founder member of the Belfast Rope Works and his son, Sir Walter Smiles represented North Down at Westminster as Member of Parliament from 1945 until his tragic death in 1953. He was drowned behind the Copeland Islands when the 'Princess Victoria' ferry boat sank. Walter was Patsie's father. She succeeded him as M.P. for the remainder of that Parliament in the by-election caused by his death.

Who was Mrs Beeton, and why did she write Household Management?

As a child I know I always imagined Mrs Beeton to be a rather dowdy old Victorian matriarch who wrote her book on Household Management after a lifetime's experience in the kitchen. On the contrary. She was only 28 when she died of puerperal fever after giving birth to her fourth son.

Isabella Mary Mayson was the eldest of a family of 21 children. She married the successful publisher Samuel Orchart Beeton in 1856 when she was 20 years old and he was 25. She was a gifted pianist and a talented 'entrepreneur' at a time when the woman's place was firmly in the home. Their marriage was a love match and a great partnership.

Isabella was immediately drawn into Sam's business activities and was soon making her debut in print with a weekly cookery column and a fashion feature. This accomplished young woman was to help expand women's horizons and change the outlook of the age.

In her preface to 'Household Management' Mrs Beeton wrote: "What moved me, in the first instance, to attempt a work like this, was the discomfort and suffering I had seen brought upon men and women by household mismanagement. I have always thought there was no more fruitful source of family discontent than a housewife's badly cooked dinners and untidy ways. Men are now so well served out of doors, – at their clubs, well ordered taverns and dinner houses, that in order to compete with the attractions of these places, a mistress must be thoroughly conversant with the theory and practice of cookery, as well as perfectly conversant with all the other arts of making and keeping 'a comfortable home'." and of course those reasons are still as relevant today as they were in 1861.

This unique book embraces a wealth of everyday and more formal recipes and covers all aspects of how to run a home. 'Household Management' was an immediate success, probably because it was the first book to deal with all aspects of housekeeping, together with exact and formal directions. Sixty thousand copies were sold in the first year, which put it in the best seller class and it continued to sell well, until there was scarcely a self-respecting kitchen in this country without a copy. Since then it has been expertly reprinted over the years and today, 156 years later, no bride's wedding list is really complete without a copy of 'Household Management'!

Mrs Bell at the Aga

I imagine that it has always been so, that the heart of any happy family home is the 'kitchen'. It is not just the prospect of food and the wonderful smells of baking that make it special, it is usually the Cooks themselves. For us, as children, it was Mrs Bell's wonderful 'surprises', and the synergy that was generated when the kitchen was filled with the laughter of friends whilst helping with the washing up. We always wished our holidays could have lasted longer.

There is something tremendously comforting about coming into a warm kitchen early in the morning when the rest of the house is sleeping and it is cold outside. Our cat thought so too as it slept curled up beside the 'Aga'. The dogs made straight for it to dry off after a wet woodland walk or a swim in the sea – and I sometimes wonder how many rescued seagulls, injured baby rabbits, abandoned kittens and vulnerable newly hatched chickens would have survived if it hadn't been for this dependable 'friend'.

If our 'Aga' could speak, it would have some most wonderful stories to tell. All the fascinating gossip it has overhead whilst people have warmed their bottoms against it over a 'cuppa', and the events it has witnessed over the generations.

The Breakfast Gong!

"The Critical period in matrimony is breakfast time."
                                                    A. P. Herbert

A squabble with a pernickety husband/wife or fratchety child can sometimes be averted by restoring their blood sugar level with

FOOD

before they have the chance to open their mouths!

"Always have a banana *within easy reach. It is instant energy."*

Muesli

This is a healthy and satisfying way to serve Muesli with a difference.

1 cup of oatflakes

2 tsp of brown sugar

Juice of $^1/_2$ lemon

1 banana chopped or mashed

1 yoghurt plain or flavoured

Juice of 2 oranges

1 grated or finely chopped apple,
raspberries or strawberries

Ground almonds

Raisins – if desired

Mix the oatflakes and the rest of the ingredients together.

Decorate with the chosen fruit and sprinkle with almonds to serve.

"Always leave a vase of freshly gathered flowers on the breakfast table and when convenient a nicely arranged bowl of fruit."

Mrs Beeton

"Portavo"

Oatmeal Porridge

Mrs Bell says that the secret of a really good porridge is to soak the oatmeal overnight. It also cuts down the cooking time in the morning. The Rt. Hon. Lord Waddington on his return as Governor of Bermuda in 1997, thought this was so good he requested a second helping!

$^1/_2$ teacup of oatmeal for each person

Enough water to cover the oats

Add a pinch of salt

Soak the oatmeal overnight.

Gently simmer on a low hotplate until the porridge is smooth and hot.

Serve with brown sugar sprinkled on top and a blob of cream.

"Early rising is one of the most essential qualities which enter into a good household. It is not only the parent of good health but of other innumerable advantages."

Mrs Beeton

Potato Bread

Potato bread is wonderful served with bacon and eggs for breakfast.

2lbs (900g) potatoes

Salt & pepper

4-6oz (115-170g) flour

Blob of butter

Boil potatoes and mash adding salt, pepper and blob of butter to taste.

Mix the flour into the mashed potatoes and knead on a floured board.

Roll out the mix to about ¼ inch thick – cut into small rounds or squares.

Cook on a hot griddle or in a heavy frying pan.

Serve for breakfast with bacon and eggs etc as an alternative to fried egg.

Mrs Bell, who made Portavo Point 'breakfasts' famous, believes this is the most important meal of the day for grown-ups as well as children. I am sure Mrs Beeton would have agreed with her.

Brown Irish Soda Bread

This recipe is particularly suitable for those on a yeast-free diet.

1^1/$_2$ lb (680g) wholemeal flour

12oz (340g) strong white flour [or
10oz (285g) strong white flour and
2oz (60g) pinhead oatmeal]

2 level tsp salt

2 level tsp sodium bicarbonate

2 level tsp sugar

4 level tsp cream of tartar

1^1/$_4$ pint (710ml) buttermilk or sour
milk

"Drink eight glasses of water every day."

Weigh out wholemeal flour and pinhead oatmeal. Put in a large mixing bowl.

Weigh out remainder of dry ingredients and sieve twice to mix, then add to brown flour. Mix well. Stir in milk all in one go!

Tip resulting large wet dough onto a well-floured board and sprinkle with flour in order to form large scone 2" thick.

Cut in four and place on preheated oiled baking sheet.

Place in pre-heated over 230°C, 450°F for 8-10 minutes.

Reduce temperature to 180°C, 350°F for 20-30 minutes.

Loaves will be cooked when they sound hollow when tapped on the bottom.

Strangford Village, Co. Down

Strangford Kedgeree

A wonderful comfort food needing no accompaniment – it can be eaten for breakfast, luncheon or supper. Rice has a finer flavour if washed in hot water, instead of cold, before cooking.

1¹/₂ lb (680g) salmon or smoked haddock (or any other cold fish)

2oz (60g) butter

Chopped parsley

Ground black pepper & salt

3 hard boiled eggs

6-8oz (170-230g) long grain brown or white rice

Small cup of single cream

Small pinch of curry powder and/or cayenne

Poach fish gently until cooked, hard boil the eggs and cook the rice until tender.

Mix the fish with the rice, chopped boiled eggs, butter, parsley, salt, black pepper and curry powder, add sufficient cream to make it moist, and serve very hot

Rice is a detoxin. For 'eczema' live for 2 weeks almost entirely on rice.

Mickey's 'Armada' Tomatoes

A great way to start the day.

1-2 tomatoes per person	Put required amount of tomatoes <u>with their skins</u> in a blender.
1 tbs olive oil	Add 1 tablespoon of olive oil per tomato (and garlic).
Pinch of salt & pepper	Season with salt & pepper to taste, blend together and serve on bread.
Sliced white bread or cut French loaf or soda bread	
$^1/_4$ clove of garlic (optional!)	There is your breakfast!

"To skin tomatoes, place them in a bowl of freshly boiled water – the skin will split and is then easily peeled off."

Tuna Fish Crumble Starter (For 8)

This is also a quick good supper dish for four people.

1 large tin of tuna drained

2 chopped hard boiled eggs

1 tbs grated onion

2-3 tbs of chopped parsley

$^3/_4$ pint (425ml) of cheese sauce

Salt & pepper

Topping mix

Grated cheese & bread crumbs

Combine all the ingredients together (except the topping mix). Place in 8 small ramekin dishes and top with the topping, leave in the fridge until needed, then put into a moderate oven for 30 minutes until brown and bubbling.

"Never take good health for granted."

Bangor Beetroot Mousse

Colour and presentation are very important. The red of the beetroot and green of the parsley make this recipe look particularly pretty in white ramekin dishes.

5 large beetroot cooked and peeled

2 pots of Philadelphia cream cheese

Lemon juice

1 tin of consommé

Pinch of nutmeg

Blend all the ingredients together in liquidiser and leave in the fridge to set.

Decorate with parsley and serve with Melba toast.

Young beet tops, with a flavour more subtle than spinach, cooked in a very little water, chopped or puréed, make an unusual vegetable alternative to accompany any main course.

Oat Soup With Cream

This is a very subtle soup; it tastes quite unlike its simple ingredients.

1 heaped tbs butter

1 large onion (finely chopped)

2 rounded tbs oatmeal (the larger flakes)

1 bay leaf

Pinch of ground nutmeg 1 tsp sugar

$1^1/_2$ pints (850ml) chicken stock

$^1/_2$ pint (285ml) cream, or half milk, half cream

Chopped parsley and a dash of cayenne pepper for garnish

Heat the butter until foaming. Add the chopped onion and cook until soft but not coloured. Add the oatmeal, bay leaf, nutmeg, sugar and salt and pepper; cook for a few minutes stirring.

Gradually add the stock, bring to the boil, lower heat and simmer, covered, for about half an hour. Liquidize, and return to the pan.

Add the cream or cream and milk and reheat to just under boiling point.

Garnish with chopped parsley and a very little cayenne pepper.

Serves 4.

"The discovery of a new recipe confers more happiness upon humanity than the discovery of a new star."
Mrs Beeton

Whitebait/Sprat

Whitebait and Sprat are the very small fry of the Herring, and are delicious eaten whole. Allow $^1/_4$ lb (115g) per person for a starter, and double the quantity for a main meal.

Heat oil for deep frying or, if preferred, a baking tray to pop in a hot oven. Dip the fish in milk and then shake them in flour in a large paper bag.

Cook until crispy.

Serve at once with lots of lemon and brown bread and butter.

"Every man who has been worth a fig in this world has had a good appetite and good taste."
Thackeray

Portaferry Potted Shrimps

Making home-made potted shrimps is a relaxing seaside occupation which all the family can enjoy.

For every pint of Shrimps allow
2oz butter
Pinch of pepper & salt and cayenne

First catch your shrimps at low tide – boil them immediately you return from the beach for about 3 minutes in salted already boiling water. Drain. Rinse with cold water and peel.

Heat a third of the butter in a pan – add seasoning. When the butter is melted stir in the shrimps (do not fry). Put into individual ramekin dishes and pour the remaining butter over the shrimps. Refrigerate to clarify the butter, then decorate with parsley and serve with toast.

"Only buy fresh shell fish if there is an 'R' in the month."

Artichoke Soup

A white soup. Season from June – October.

2-3lbs (910g-1.37kg) Jerusalem Artichokes

1lb (450g) Potatoes

2-3 onions

$^1/_2$ – $^3/_4$ pints (285-425ml) milk

Butter

Salt & pepper

Peel artichokes. Chop onions and 'sweat' them with the artichokes in butter in a large saucepan. Add the stock and milk. Season well and simmer until soft. Peel and cook potatoes.

Blend altogether in a liquidiser. If too thick thin down with milk or cream.

Serve hot with a dollop of cream, chopped chives or parsley, or fried croutons.

"Vegetable soup is improved by a handful of finely chopped nettles which are full of the vitamins and minerals so beneficial for gout and arthritis."

Stilton Soup

This is a wonderfully aromatic and interesting soup, particularly after Christmas when there maybe Stilton left-overs.

1½ oz (40g) butter or margarine

1 large onion

2oz (55g) plain flour

¾ pint (425ml) good chicken stock

1 bay leaf

1 sprig thyme

8oz (225g) Stilton cheese crumbled

¾ pint (425ml) milk

4 tbs double cream

Salt & freshly ground pepper

Flat leaf parsley to garnish

4 tbs chopped walnuts

Melt the butter or margarine in a saucepan, add the chopped onions and sauté until soft. Stir in the flour and allow to cook for 2 minutes.

Gradually add in the chicken stock stirring constantly. Add the bay leaf, thyme, and salt & pepper to taste. Bring to the boil and simmer for 2 minutes.

Remove the herbs and add the crumbled stilton into the soup. Cook for 5 minutes – stir in cream.

Pour into a soup tureen and garnish with chopped parsley and walnuts.

Serves 4.

"The way to a man's heart is through his stomach."

Mrs Beeton

Donaghadee Lighthouse, Co. Down

Donaghadee Eggs

A very good supper dish – serves six

1 egg per person	Place well-greased ramekin dishes, one per person, in the oven to butter.
1 slice ham or salami (chopped finely)	
	Add chopped tomatoes and onions, ham, or best of all salami.
2 tomatoes (chopped finely)	Mix with a few cooked peas.
1 onion (chopped finely)	Place in a moderate over for 5 minutes
Cooked peas	When hot, break a whole egg on top of each ramekin.
Salt and pepper	Add salt and pepper and a little cream
Parsley	Cook in a moderate oven, ensuring yolk remains soft.
Blob of cream for each ramekin	Decorate with parsley and serve.

"To test an egg for freshness, place it in a basin of water. If it is fresh it will sink, if it is not so fresh but still edible, it sinks a short distance; and if it is stale it will float on the water."

Sardine Surprise

This also makes an excellent savoury picnic paté or 'snack' eaten directly from a Tupperware pot with a spoon for the hungry fisherman awaiting his catch!

2 tins of sardines

Worcestershire sauce

Salt & black pepper

Remove backbones from larger sardines – mash sardines in a round bowl and mix in liberal dollops of Worcestershire sauce. Add lots of black pepper.

Spread on toast or fried bread and either keep warm in a slow oven or grill and serve.

"For sea sickness – take as much cayenne pepper as you can possibly bear in a basin of hot soup and all sea sickness and nausea will disappear."

Cassandra, Countess of Rosse's Housekeeper, 1870

Mackerel With Gooseberry Sauce

There are two ways to cook mackerel fillets quickly and simply – either bake them or fry them. They are dramatically at their best eaten on the day they are caught.

2 large mackerel

1 tbs seasoned flour

1oz (30g) margarine

Tomatoes

$^1/_2$ lb (225g) gooseberries

$^1/_4$ level tsp grated nutmeg

Squeeze of lemon

Dip each fillet in seasoned flour. Melt margarine in bottom of the grill pan and add fillets – brush with melted fat and squeeze of lemon and grill for 8-10 minutes, turning once.

Cut the tomatoes and grill at the same time.

Meanwhile prepare the gooseberries, stew in a very little water, then purée. Stir in grated nutmeg and reheat (reduce if necessary).

Serve the fillets on hot dish, garnished with tomatoes and serve sauce separately. This unusual sauce enhances most plain white fish.

Mackerel is good with a fruity salad, ie, avocados, orange & chicory – with not too much oily dressing.

"The voracity of the mackerel is very great and, from their immense numbers, they are bold in attacking objects of which they might otherwise be expected to have wholesome dread."

Household Management

Building a fire on the beach to barbecue.

Sea Bass or Sea Trout with Seaweed

A very old method of cooking fish is to poach or steam the fresh catch over seaweed in the sand, and we sometimes did this as children. This gives a wonderful flavour, but the fish must be absolutely fresh and the seaweed well washed.

1 large bunch freshly gathered dulse or seaweed, well washed

1 Sea Bass or Sea Trout

Lemon juice

Salt & freshly ground black pepper

2 sprigs thyme

1 sprig fennel

Make a fire made in a small hole dug in the sand. When the flames die down cover with seaweed. Place fish on top to cook for about ½ hour.

This is a difficult dish to make at home unless you live near the sea. Watercress or sorrel can also be used instead of seaweed and also produces a fine dish, with a wonderful aroma. Any thick white fish can replace the seabass.

An alternative method of cooking – lay half the seaweed (or watercress) in an enamelled oval heatproof pot, large enough to hold the fish. Rub the fish with lemon juice inside and out, season and lay on top of the seaweed. Place the sprigs of herbs on top, then put the rest of the seaweed over the fish. Add the warmed liquid to the pan, cover and cook over a fairly high heat for half an hour or until the fish will come easily off the bone.

Serve with lots of melted butter.

Bear's Recipe for Skinning & Filleting A Trout

This method is ideal for most fish and will enable you to produce a fillet of trout with no bones or skin and without getting involved with any gutting at all. It is designed to save time and leaves no mess.

A VERY SHARP KNIFE IS CRUCIAL

With your very sharp knife, cut firmly down vertically beside the fish's head as deep as the backbone only. Then cut the flesh away along the length of the backbone until you reach the tail. <u>It is important not to cut the tail off</u>. Flip this cut fillet over on its back so the skin is on the bottom and the flesh facing you on the top. Then with the side of the knife, cut under the fillet between the flesh and skin until the fillet comes away from the skin, (still leave the skin attached to the tail). Turn the fish over and repeat on the other side to produce 2 skinless, boneless fillets of trout.

Grill with butter, salt and pepper and lots of lemon juice, dill, thyme and parsley

"A general rule in choosing fish, a proof of freshness and goodness in most fishes is their being covered with scales; for, if deficient in this respect, it is a sign of their being stale, or having been ill-used."
Household Management – 1861

Haddock Soufflé

1 medium smoked haddock per person

6oz (170g) butter

$^1/_2$ pint (285ml) double cream

milk

1 tbs flour

5 eggs

Poach and flake fish into buttered oven-proof dish. Cover with 4 oz butter and cream (keep warm). Mix 2 oz butter and flour – mix in egg yolks – mix in beaten egg whites then pour over fish from outside in.

Bake for 20 minutes at 350°F or Gas 3.

"When poaching eggs add a teaspoon of vinegar to the water. This helps to set the white and keep it from spreading."

Birdwatching over the Copeland Islands.

Copeland Island 'Kipper Paté'

This same recipe can also be made using off-cuts of smoked salmon pieces.

2 kipper fillets – cooked & boned

8oz (225g) butter

Cream

Juice of 1 lemon

Salt & pepper

1 lemon

Skin and bone kipper. Place in a liquidiser. Add melted butter and blend until smooth, add a dash of cream – season.

Pour into a pate dish and chill – when cold pour over clarified butter and leave in fridge to harden.

Decorate with slices of lemon and parsley sprigs.

Serve with warm toast.

"Simple cooking cannot be trusted to a simple cook."

Countess Morphe

Crab Cakes

Breakfast, luncheon or supper – these are a marvellous treat.

1 large fresh cooked and prepared crab (white and brown meat)

4 potatoes

1 small onion

1 egg

Pinch of cayenne

Salt & pepper

Chopped parsley

Fresh white breadcrumbs – as required

Boil and mash the potatoes and place in a large bowl. Grate the onion, add crab meat, salt, pepper, cayenne and parsley. Beat the egg and add to the mixture. Add enough breadcrumbs to make a dough. Divide into 3" round balls. Lightly roll in flour and gently flatten out.

Fry on a medium heat with a little oil until golden.

Serve with cold tomato sauce or hot parsley sauce.

"Early rising is one of the most essential qualities that enter into household management."
Mrs Beeton

Monkfish Piperade

This is an ideal luncheon dish served with a green salad.

1¹/₂ lb (680g) monkfish – skinned and filleted

2 onions – sliced thinly

Peppers – 1 green, 1 red and 1 yellow – deseeded and cut into thin strips

2 cloves of garlic – crushed

7¹/₂ oz (215g) tin chopped tomatoes

2–3 tbs olive oil

1 small french stick

Oil for frying

Salt & freshly ground black pepper

"Clean as you go as muddle leads to muddle."

Mrs Beeton

Place a saucepan on to simmer and add the olive oil and onions. Soften the onions then add the crushed garlic.

Allow to cook for 2-3 minutes then add the tinned tomatoes and sliced peppers. Cook until the peppers have softened and the sauce has reduced slightly. Season to taste.

Place the fillets of monkfish into a well buttered overproof dish and spoon the piperade over the fish.

Place in a moderate oven and cook for 20-30 minutes until the fish becomes tender.

Cut french bread and fry in oil until golden brown and serve around the piperade.

Serves 4.

Fish Pie

Of all the fish pie recipes, this one was the family's favourite. It is so quick and easy to make and turns into wonderful home-made fish cakes for either breakfast, or supper served with minted fresh garden peas and home-made tomato ketchup.

2lbs (900g) cod or haddock

2lbs (900g) potatoes (to boil and mash) [to every 1lb (450g) mashed potato allow 1 oz (30g) butter]

Large bunch parsley

1 pint (570ml) milk

Added water for fish stock

Salt & pepper

Poach the fish in water with a little milk and simmer until cooked. When cooked drain and keep the stock liquid.

Make a fairly sloppy parsley sauce with the basic white sauce recipe – using up the remains of milk and the fish stock.

Add salt and pepper to taste.

Meanwhile, boil and mash the potatoes adding butter to flavour. Mix the potatoes, fish and parsley sauce (see recipe on page 40) altogether and place in a pie or casserole dish.

Decorate with sliced tomatoes and parsley – and more mashed potato on top if desired.

When mashing potatoes allow 1lb (450g) potato for every 3 people.

Baked Onions

Serve as an alternative to a baked potato. They are wonderful with a blob of cottage cheese on top with a salad, or plain with a Sunday joint.

1 large onion per person

Trim the base if necessary so they will stand upright, but do not peel – make a horizontal and vertical cut to open onions a little. Stand the onions in a roasting tin, wrapped in foil, and pour in about 2.5cm/1 inch of hot water. Bake until cooked. (Do not overcook.)

"Like the cabbage, this plant was erected into an object of worship by the Idolatrous Egyptians 2000 years before the Christian era, when it was introduced to England has not been ascertained, but it has long been esteemed as a favourite seasoning plant to various dishes."
Household Management

Kalcannon

The Irish make this with Seakale, but it is just as good with cabbage.
Served with cooked ham and home-made chutney, this makes a satisfying lunch or supper.

$1\frac{1}{4}$ lb (570g) green cabbage, finely chopped

1 small leek finely chopped

$2\frac{1}{2}$-5 fl oz (75-150ml) milk

$1\frac{1}{4}$ lb (570g) potatoes

Salt and pepper

Pinch of grated nutmeg

2oz (60g) melted butter

Simmer the cabbage and leeks in just enough milk to cover until soft with the nutmeg.

Boil and mash the potatoes – season.

Add the cabbage and leek mixture.

Place in a deep warm serving dish – make a well in the centre and pour in the butter.

"The potato came from Virginia, USA in 1586 and was first planted by Sir Walter Raleigh on his estate of Yourghal near Cork in Ireland."

Household Management

Vegetarian Cheese Pie

3 large potatoes

1 large onion

1 leek

1 large grated carrot

1/2 tsp mixed herbs

3/4 pint (425ml) white sauce

6oz (170g) grated Cheddar cheese

Salt & black pepper

1 pkt plain crisps

Grease a 2½ pint (1.5l) casserole. Peel and slice potatoes thinly. Chop onions and slice leeks cross-wise. Layer potatoes, onions, leeks and carrots in the dish.

Make ¾ pint (425ml) of white sauce and to this add the grated cheese, salt, pepper and herbs.

Cover and bake in over for 2½ hours at 300°F.

During the last 10 minutes of the cooking remove lid and sprinkle broken crisps over the top.

"The garden carrot was introduced in the reign of Queen Elizabeth I and was, at first, so highly esteemed that the ladies wore leaves of it in their head-dresses. It is of great value in the culinary art, particularly for soups and stews."

Household Management

Yorkshire Pudding

As Patsie's great grandfather, Samuel Smiles, author of '*Self Help*', '*Character*' and '*Thrift*', and her grandson-in-law are both Yorkshire men, I felt it appropriate to include a recipe for Yorkshire Pudding.

Yorkshire, the largest and one of the most beautiful counties in England, is also one of it's bleakest. The prosperity of it's industry over generations is not just from iron, steel and textiles, but the industry of it's people. Because Yorkshire people work hard – they have always had to – they have good appetites, and they believe in enjoying themselves when work is done. And, because they are thrifty and ingenious, they make the best use of their materials. From all these ingredients the Yorkshire Pudding was born.

Although Yorkshire pudding is a batter mix, it is not a stodge. A partner to roast beef in England; in Yorkshire, it's first function is to allay the pangs of hunger felt by those who have worked hard, and its batter base is used with a wide variety of satisfying savoury and sweet fillings. To savour the full excellence of this pudding, it is not enough to roast the beef and bake the batter, we should do it the Yorkshire way!

Yorkshire Pudding

"Yorkshire women are reputed to be the best cooks in England, and Yorkshire men are epicures, so there you have the warranty for the excellence of Yorkshire Pudding."

2 eggs

6oz (170g) PLAIN flour (definitely NOT self-raising flour)

$1/2$ pint (285ml) of milk

$1/2$ tsp salt

Sieve the flour and make a well in the middle of the bowl. Drop in the eggs, milk and salt and beat all together. Leave to sit in a cool place for 1 hour if possible. Just before cooking give the mix another good beat.

Roast a large joint (small ones are apt to shrivel) in a hot oven on the open grid bars of the oven shelf. (Do not stand in a baking tray). About 6 inches below this grid have another shelf and on it a roasting pad to catch all the falls from the meat.

20 minutes before serving remove the drip pan, drain the fat and skim away the bits. Pour some of the remaining fat back into the roasting pan. Give the Yorkshire Pudding mix its final beat and pour into the roasting tin. Return to the oven and bake under the joint where it will absorb all the drips from it.

"The secret of a successful Yorkshire Pudding is really hot fat in a really hot oven."

Parsley Sauce

To preserve parsley for sauces or decoration, gather, wash and dry. When crisp, rub through a sieve – put in bottle. It will keep its colour to garnish dishes."

28fl oz (800ml) milk

1 large bunch of parsley finely chopped

1½ oz (40g) butter

1oz (30g) flour

Salt & pepper

Melt butter in a saucepan, mix in the flour and cook over a gentle heat stirring until it starts to smell nutty and warm.

Take care not to let it burn or go beyond a pale biscuit colour. Stir in the milk with a wooden spoon.

Bring the sauce gently almost to the boil again, add the chopped parsley then turn down the heat so that the sauce cooks slowly, barely bubbling for a few minutes. Stir from time to time and add salt and pepper to taste.

"Among the Greeks a crown of parsley was awarded in the Olympic games. This beautiful herb was pronounced the emblem of joy and festivity. The curled is best and, from its leaf, has a beautiful appearance on a dish as a garnish"

Household Management

Mrs Bell's Special Boiled Chicken with vegetables and parsley sauce

This is all goodness, and the leftover juice and stock makes wonderful SOUP. The juice is particularly nourishing for invalids recovering from illness who may have no appetite for food.

1 large chicken

3 onions

4 carrots

1 cup of pearl barley

1 cup of lentils

2 bay leaves

Salt & pepper

Root vegetables (optional)
eg parsnip, swede, turnip

Put chicken together with all the ingredients in a saucepan or slow cooker and cook until chicken is tender and the vegetables are cooked.

Remove flesh from carcass and put back into the casserole dish with the vegetables.

Serve in its own juice with parsley sauce.

"Always respond to R.S.V.P. invitations promptly. If there is a telephone number, call. If not, write a note."

Braised Rabbit

Rabbit is a great food for Country people. To make this recipe extra special, add red wine and marmalade.

1 rabbit, skinned & jointed

3 tbs oil

1 large onion, sliced

3-4 carrots

Flour (to coat)

Pinch of powdered marjoram

Salt & pepper

1 pint (570ml) chicken stock or half stock, half cider

Pat the joints dry. Heat oil and fry joints on each side until golden brown. Lift them out and put them in a casserole. In the same oil lightly fry vegetables. Add marjoram, salt and pepper. Sprinkle in a little flour and stir. Add the stock gradually, stirring until smooth. Pour over rabbit and cover and cook in a moderate oven for ½ hour. Then lower heat and cook for a further 1½ hours.

This braise can also be used for a delicious Rabbit Pie. Add 2-3 rashers of chopped bacon – cover with shortcrust pastry and cook for ½ hour.

"To invite a person into your house is to take charge of his happiness for as long as he is under your roof."
Brillat Savarin

Lara's 'Crisis' Chicken

This takes two minutes and tastes as good as if you have been cooking all day. (Mrs Beeton might well turn in her grave!)

4 chicken breasts

2 tins of any condensed soup (preferably chicken!)

Pepper & salt

Mixed herbs to taste

Dash of 'Harveys' Sauce

1-2 bags of potato crisps

Gratcd cheese

Lay chicken breasts in base of oven-proof dish. Pour over 2 tins of condensed soup and season.

Crumble the potato crisps over the chicken and top with grated cheese.

Cook at moderate heat for 45 minutes.

Serves 4.

"Don't slave away cooking something for hours if you can do it in minutes."
Lara Fawcett

Downpatrick Cathedral, Co. Down

Downpatrick Irish Stew

2lb (900g) best end of neck of lamb or lamb cutlets (1 per person)

1lb (450g) onions

1lb (450g) carrots

3lb (1.3kg) potatoes

$1^1/_2$ pt (850ml) stock or water

2 bay leaves

Parsley

Salt and pepper

Cut the meat into neat cutlets and trim off the surplus fat.

Arrange in a casserole dish layers of meat, thinly sliced onions, seasoning, and half of the potatoes cut in slices.

Add stock or water just to cover and simmer gently for $1^1/_2$ hours.

Add the rest of the potatoes cut to a uniform size to improve the appearance of the top. Cook gently in the steam for $^1/_2$ hour longer.

Serve the meat in the centre of a hot dish and arrange the potatoes around the edge. Pour the liquid over the meat and sprinkle with finely chopped parsley.

"A spoonful of brown sugar to any mince, stew or gravy stock improves the flavour."

Home-Made Tomato Sauce

Serve as a better alternative to ketchup. It can be used with pasta or meatballs or served over cod or any fish.

4lbs (1.82kg) ripe tomatoes, peeled & chopped

3 tsp allspice

3 onions

3 cloves of garlic

$1/2$ cup sugar

3 tbs basil

1 tbs oregano

1 tbs lemon mint thyme

2 cups cider vinegar

$1/2$ tsp black pepper

Place tomatoes in saucepan with spices – add onions, garlic and simmer for 30 minutes or until thickened.

Stir in remaining ingredients until mixture reaches a sauce consistency.

Put in a bottle. This mixture freezes well.

"There is no more fruitful source of discontent than a housewife's badly cooked dinner and untidy ways."
Mrs Beeton

Food for thought .....

*"Do not, unless invited, take pet dogs into another house.
There are people who have a great aversion to animals, and
there is always the chance of the animal breaking something.
Moreover, the people themselves may have a dog –
and anything may happen."*

Isobella Beeton
Household Management

Dieting under Stress

For those of you who feel (or know) that you have over-indulged during the holiday season, the following diet is designed to help you cope with the stress that builds up during the day:

BREAKFAST

½ grapefruit, 1 slice wholemeal toast, 3 oz skimmed milk

LUNCH

4 oz lean boiled chicken breast, 1 cup steamed spinach, 1 cup herbal tea, 1 chocolate digestive biscuit.

MID-AFTERNOON SNACK

Rest of biscuits in packet, 2 pints chocolate-chip ice-cream, 1 jar hot fudge sauce with nuts, cherries and fresh cream.

DINNER

2 loaves garlic bread with cheese, 1 large sausage pizza, 4 cans or party pack of lager, 3 Twix or Mars Bars.

LATE EVENING SNACK

Entire Black Forest gâteau.

Rules

1. If you eat something and no-one sees you eat it, it has no calories.

2. If you drink a Diet Coke with a Mars Bar, the calories of the Mars Bar are cancelled out by the Diet Coke.

3. When you eat with someone else, the calories don't count, if you don't eat more than they do.

4. Food used for medicinal purposes never count – such as hot chocolate, brandy, toast and honey.

5. If you fatten up everyone around you, you look thinner.

6. Movie related foods do not have additional calories because they are part of the whole entertainment package and not part of one's personal fuel – such as milkshakes, Murray Mints and Mars Bars.

7. Broken biscuits contain no calories – breaking causes calorie leakage.

8. Things licked off knives and teaspoons have no calories if you are in the process of preparing something.

9. Foods of the same colour have the same number of calories, eg, spinach and mint ice cream or mushrooms and white chocolate.

The moral of this diet is: "If you want to keep your figure, <u>STOP</u> before you become overstressed!"

Honey and Lavender Ice-Cream

An unusual ice-cream with a delicate flavour.

1 tbs dried lavender

2 tbs honey

1 pint (570ml/2¹/₂ cups) cream

1 pint (570ml/2¹/₂ cups) custard

Make an infusion with the lavender and 2 tablespoons of water – strain carefully into a small bowl. Add the honey and mix together.

Add the cream and custard and freeze in an ice-cream machine.

"Bunches of lavender hanging in the kitchen helps deter the flies."

Queen Of Puddings

To vary this recipe use a tin of apricots together with apricot jam.

1 pint (570ml) of milk

5oz (140g) bread crumbs

2 eggs

1oz (30g) butter

1 lemon (rind and juice)

2oz (60g) sugar

Raspberry or strawberry jam
(preferably home-made)

Boil the milk with the lemon rind (grated). Add the breadcrumbs and cook for a few minutes.

Cool the mixture, and then add the sugar, butter and egg yolks and mix together.

Put into a buttered oven-proof dish and bake in a cool oven for about $\frac{1}{2}$ hour.

Remove from oven and spread jam liberally over the pudding.

Make a meringue with the stiffly beaten egg white, pile on top and return to a hot oven and bake until crisp.

Serve immediately with cream.

"Surprise a new neighbour with one of your favourite home-made dishes, and give them the recipe."

Blackcurrant Leaf Sorbet

Herbalists have believed in the power of raspberry leaves and blackcurrant leaves for centuries, particularly during pregnancy. They have properties that are believed to protect against miscarriage – Cows eat them if they can get them when in calf.

8oz (225g) caster sugar

1 pint (570ml) water

3 handfuls of small blackcurrant leaves

Grated rind and juice of a lemon

2 egg whites

Place the sugar and water in a saucepan, heat gently until dissolved, then boil for 10 minutes. Add the blackcurrant leaves and lemon rind and leave to cool.

Liquidize the leaves and strain.

Pour the cold liquid into a bowl and add the lemon juice until you can detect a real tang. Whisk the egg whites until stiff and fold them into the mixture.

If you don't have an ice-cream maker, beat the mixture. After a couple of hours of freezing beat the mixture again and re-freeze.

Serve with walnut or almond biscuits.

"Give me the luxuries of life and I will willingly do without the necessities."
Frank Lloyd-Wright

Light & Luscious Lemon Mousse Ice-Cream

8 eggs

$^1/_2$ pint (285ml) double cream

6oz (170g) caster sugar

8 meringue nests

Grated rind and juice of 1 lemon

Separate egg yolks and whites – whisk yolks together and put on one side.

Whisk egg whites adding caster sugar. Whip cream until thick. Combine all together with the meringue nest lightly crushed, lemon rind and juice.

Place in suitable freezer trays or bowls until frozen.

"I feel a recipe is only a theme, which an intelligent cook can play each time with a variation."
Madame Benoit

Yummy Bananas

This is so easy and so tasty and always goes down well. Serve it piping hot with cream or as a filling for pancakes.

4 large bananas (not too ripe yet not too green)

4oz (115g) butter

2 tbs of dark rum (or brandy if preferred)

2oz (60g) soft brown sugar

Melt the butter in a frying pan. Add the peeled bananas and fry for 3-5 minutes until they begin to soften.

Add sugar and rum and cook until liquid bubbles.

Divide into 4 and serve at once with thick cream.

"Accept every invitation unless you have a good reason not to, you never know who you may meet."

Gooseberry Fool

This also makes a delicious and unusual ice-cream.

1lb (450g) gooseberries

4oz (115g) sugar

1 tbs elderflower cordial (optional)

$^{1}/_{2}$ pint (285ml) double cream or custard

Stew gooseberries with the sugar. Liquidize them or sieve them then mix together with cream and blend together.

Serve in brandy snap baskets or in small bowls with a blob of cream or crumbled ginger nut biscuits to decorate.

"Food that is not well relished cannot be well digested."

Mrs Beeton

Caramel Custard

For the Caramel

3oz (85g) sugar

$^1/_4$ pint (140ml) water

For the Custard

2 whole eggs

2 egg yolks

$^2/_3$ tbs sugar

1 pint (570ml) milk

A few drops of vanilla essence

Sugar to taste

"Presentation is half the art of cooking."

Place the sugar into a saucepan with a little water and allow to dissolve. When it begins to change colour stir carefully until it is a good brown colour, then pour into a warmed, medium sized, oval glass ovenproof dish and coat the bottom and sides with the caramel.

The Custard

Beat the eggs, yolk, sugar and vanilla together. Heat the milk and pour over the egg mixture. Stir well and then pour into the prepared dish.

Stand dish in a roasting tin containing hot water, and place in a moderate oven until set. Remove from the heat and leave until cold. Serve straight from the dish with cream.

Garnish with strawberries and mint leaves.

Rice Pudding

Mr Cyril Lord always asked for this pudding.
Nutmeg is particularly good with milky puddings.

3-4 tbs of pudding rice

2-3 tbs of sugar

$1^1/_2$ -2 pints (850ml-1.2l) milk

1 small tin of 'Ideal' milk

Pinch of salt

Pinch of nutmeg

Put rice and pinch of salt into a large saucepan and cover with water.

Simmer until the rice is soft. Add the milk and sugar and simmer until most of the milk is absorbed into the rice, add the Ideal (evaporated) milk and put the mixture into a greased pie dish.

Place in a moderate over and bake until lightly browned.

Serve with any stewed fruit and cream or a good raspberry jam.

"When milk puddings first became popular in the 18th century, they were made with cream, cooked with fortified wines and extravagantly filled with sultanas and currents. You can use herbs and spices in sweet dishes as well as savoury ones."

'Delicious' Pudding

Sir David Frost liked this pudding. He asked for the recipe.

1 cup sugar	Cream sugar and butter together, add lemon juice and grated rind, then add yolks of eggs and flour, then stir in the milk.
1 tbs butter	Beat egg whites then gently fold into mixture.
1 heaped tbs flour	Put into oven-proof dish.
1½ cups of milk	Place dish in a pan of hot water, and bake in a slow oven for about ¾-1 hour.
1 lemon (juice and rind)	(If doubling this recipe – only use two cups of milk.)
2 eggs	
Pinch of salt	

"Compliment the meal when you are a guest in someone's house."

Irish Coffee Ice Cream

4 egg yolks

³/4 cup caster sugar

2 x 300ml cartons double cream

3 tsp instant coffee powder

2 tbs hot water

¹/3 cup of Irish Whisky

Beat egg yolks and sugar in small bowl with electric mixer until light and fluffy. Heat cream in pan until almost boiling. With mixer operating gradually beat in coffee combined with water then the whisky. When all mixed together pour into freezer trays or freeze-proof bowl – cover with foil and freeze for several hours until partly frozen. Chop ice-cream roughly. Return to small bowl of mixer, mixing until smooth. Return to ice-trays or bowl and cover with foil. Place in freezer until set.

Serve with fruit and whipped cream if desired.

"Good communication is as stimulating as black coffee."
Anne Morrow Lindurgh

Lemon Curd

4oz (115g) butter

1lb (450g) caster sugar

4 eggs

2 lemons (rind and juice)

Put butter, sugar grated lemon rind and juice into a large double saucepan and melt all together slowly.

Stir in the beaten eggs and boil gently – keep stirring until the curd coats the back of your wooden spoon.

Pot and cover.

"If a lemon is beaten well before squeezing, double the juice is obtained."

Rose's Apple And Ginger Chutney

Children enjoy this as a 'spread' in sandwiches.

1lb (450g) onions, minced or chopped

5lb (2.25kg) cooking apples, minced or chopped

2 level tsp ground ginger

1-2 level tsp salt

1^{1}/$_{2}$ lb (680g) sugar

^{3}/$_{4}$ -1 pint (425-570ml) vinegar (spiced pickling vinegar)

Cook onions in covered pad with ½ pint of water for 20 minutes. Add apples, ginger and salt. Cook for about 30 minutes until tender – you may need a little vinegar to prevent burning.

Add the sugar and the rest of the vinegar and stir well. Continue to boil gently with the lid off, until the chutney is thick, and no liquid vinegar remains.

When preserving foods it is best to use stainless steel pans – do NOT use aluminium, brass or copper pans.

Children's Chocolate Cake

This is a wartime recipe originally made with lard. We make it now with butter and it is absolutely delicious.

1 breakfast cup (6 oz) of flour
$^3/_4$ breakfast cup (4 oz) of sugar
2 tbs cocoa
$^3/_4$ cup (284 ml) buttermilk or soured milk
1 heaped tsp baking powder
1 level tsp baking soda
2oz (60g) butter
Filling and topping
6oz (170g) sugar
3oz (85g) butter
1 tbs cocoa
2 tbs milk
1 tbs margarine/butter

Mix the dry ingredients together, then rub in the butter.

Mix to sponge consistency with the buttermilk. Line two 7" sandwich tins with greaseproof paper.

Bake in moderate oven 350˚F/175˚C for 20 minutes.

Mix all the ingredient together – spread in sponge and dust with sugar.

"Frugality and economy are home virtues without which no household can prosper."
Mrs Beeton

The Great Mrs Beeton

This is an extract taken from an article written in 'The Star' 17th February, 1932 by Isobella's half-sister, Mrs Lucy Smiles, who was then living in Belfast.

There are people still living in Epsom who remember a mid-Victorian family with very intricate relationships. Henry Dorling, a widower with four children, married Elizabeth Mayson, a widow with four children, and had thirteen more children. Henry Dorling owned the Grand Stand at the time, and printed the cards for the race meetings. His name is still remembered – "Dorling's Correct Card".

The first to be married of this amazing family was Isabella Mayson, now known to thousands of readers as "Mrs Beeton". She was married in June 1856 at Epsom Parish Church to Samuel Orchart Beeton, and I was the principal bridesmaid at the wedding.

She had eight bridesmaids. We two children (Jessie Beeton and I) walked first in white embroidered muslin, and hats and beige boots. I got my first corn from those boots. Three of the grown-up bridesmaids wore pale green, and three mauve silk – all with three-tiered skirts. Their bonnets had little flowers resting on the hair in front.

The bride? She wore a bonnet, too, and her white silk frock was flounced to the waist. But I don't remember her dress as well as my own boots. Her petticoat was beautiful. Each flounce was of a different design, and had been embroidered by one of her sisters. It was a gorgeous day, just after the summer meeting, and the wedding breakfast was given in the salon at the Grand Stand. I can still remember how picturesque the guests looked out on the course in front – the big skirts and the fringed parasols. They went to Paris for their honeymoon, driving off in a carriage and pair to Reigate (nine miles) to catch the Folkestone train. The only present I can remember is the white piano that my father gave her. She had been a pupil of Sir Julius Benedict and played uncommonly well.

The Beeton's first home was at 2 Chandos Villas, Pinner. I remember staying with them there in 1858. I liked being with them. I can still remember how nicely my supper-tray was set out, when it was brought up to me, for I was only a child and went early to bed.

Mrs Beeton's Supper

Sam's work was in Fleet Street, and he used to catch the last train down from town. He missed it once, and had to walk the whole way home. He was never home before midnight, but no matter how late he was, a hot supper was waiting for him. I can still remember how good it smelt. On Sunday we didn't go to church, which I thought very extraordinary. We walked, instead, to Harrow-on-the-Hill, more extraordinary. The house was small, but properly staffed. There were two maids, and I remember Isabella outside with the gardener arranging about the rhododendrons being planted.

I never remember her idle. She was busy translating French stories when I was there, as well as testing the recipes for her cookery book. When she came back from school in Heidelberg, she had had lessons in pastry-making from the Epsom confectioner. This was supposed to be ultra modern, and 'not quite nice'.

Different people gave their recipes for the book. That for Baroness Pudding (a suet pudding without eggs, and with a plethora of raisins) was given by the Baroness de Tessier, who lived in Epsom. No recipe went into the book without a successful trial, and No 2 Chandos Villas was the scene of many experiments and some failures. I remember Isabella coming out of the kitchen one day. "This won't do at all." She said, and gave me the cake, that had turned out like a biscuit. I thought it very good. It had currants in it.

A Famous Soup

It was a hard winter that year, and the poor children of the neighbourhood came regularly with their cans for soup. Each week they brought bigger cans. The soup was made of oxhead, and appears in her book under the title of '*Useful Soup for Benevolent Purposes*'. In fact Mrs Beeton's book of cookery was first brought out to meet the demand for an economical cookery book, and many of the soup recipes were for those cheap soups used in France and Germany – cabbage soup, bread soup, soup made from pea pods – but they are too economical for us nowadays.

To casually dismiss Mrs Beeton as extravagant is ridiculous, but not more ridiculous than to describe S.O. Beeton as "husband of Mrs Beeton". He was a well-known publisher (I remember being at his offices in the Strand to see Queen Alexandra's arrival in London in the summer of 1863). The best-known work he published was '*Uncle Tom's Cabin*', he made a fortune out of that and lost it bringing out the sequel – '*Dred*', I think it was called.

Death at 29
'*Beeton's Dictionary of Useful Information*', compiled by him, was the source of many of the interesting notes to be found in the original editions of the cookery book. Among the numerous journals that he brought out was one called '*The English-woman's Domestic Magazine*', to which Isabella contributed translations and fashion articles. She got her clothes in Paris, and I well remember how fashionable she always looked. '*The English-woman's Domestic Magazine*' was the first paper to issue paper patterns to its readers, Isabella, buying the model in Paris, the paper patterns being cut out in London. It was her husband's idea, of course. He was a pioneer in all sorts of ways, and had the fate of all pioneers – he sowed and others reaped. But the story of Isabella isn't complete without telling something of her husband's story.

What else did she write? Well, she died when she was 29, and she had had four children and had compiled her cookery book. There was no time for more.

Thrift .....

Mrs Beeton's advocacy of 'frugality and economy' may seem surprising when she earned herself the reputation of being rather extravagant – Take a dozen eggs for this, a quart of wine for that;

But butter, eggs, cheese and vegetables were cheap when she was writing 'Household Management'. It was the meat that was expensive, and she was constantly recommending cheaper more nutritious cuts. Moreover, she was writing for large households of over 15 people. She was, in fact, extremely budget conscious, forever urging her readers to be frugal and practice good management of money and resources.

Mrs Beeton also recommended watching the budget when choosing clothes too.
"It is well that the buyer considers these things":

1. That it is not too expensive for her purse

2. That its colour harmonise with her complexion and its size and pattern with her figure.

3. That its tint allows of its being worn with the other garments she possesses.

Whilst on this theme, I am reminded of Patsie's advice to me, "Never buy a dress if it will look alright with jewellery" and "If in doubt, LEAVE OFF."

'Savoury' Bread Pudding

This is a good emergency recipe to keep up one's sleeve as the ingredients are usually in most people's store cupboard. For a large number of people the quantities can be increased. This recipe is for four people.

4 slices of buttered bread	Place bread into a well greased oven-proof dish.
4 eggs	Mix eggs and milk and cream together, season to taste.
$1/_4$ pint (140ml) milk	Pour over bread and cover with the grated cheese.
2 tbs of cream	Cook in moderate oven for $3/_4$-1 hour.
4oz (115g) grated cheese (mature cheddar is best)	Optional topping – tomato or anchovies.
Salt & pepper	Serve with a green salad.

"Care should be taken by the hostess in the selection of the invited guests that they should be suited to each other."

Mrs Beeton

Mascarpone Cream

This is a wonderful accompaniment to any fresh or stewed fruit pudding.

4 rounded tbs Mascarpone

4 rounded tbs fromage frais

A few drops of vanilla extract

1 dessertspoon caster sugar

Beat all ingredients thoroughly

"My grandmother, Lady Masserene, was advised by her doctor as a young girl to spend one day a week in bed. She thought this was a great idea and lived to be 104."

Mary Fagan

Peaches Portavo

This is quick and easy. Fresh peaches, skinned and served with a puréed raspberry sauce, make a refreshing and non-fattening alternative to this recipe.

1 peach per person

Ratafia biscuits

Brown sugar

Melted butter

Amaretta liqueur

Halve the peaches and remove the stone, put in an oven-proof dish.

Fill the centre with crushed biscuits and brown sugar.

Melt butter and pour over the peach halves, add the liqueur and cook in a hot oven for about 10 minutes.

Serve with whipped cream or crème fraiche.

"Nothing lovelier can be found in women than to study household good."
Milton

Scrabo Tower, Co. Down

Black Treacle Mousse

This 'scrummy' mousse goes well with an orange compote.

3 eggs (separated)

3 heaped tbs caster sugar

3 tbs water

2 tbs black treacle

10fl oz (285ml) whipping cream

3 tsp gelatine

2oz (60g) chopped nuts

Beat egg yolks and sugar together until thick and creamy, then add the black treacle and water and heat for a further 2 minutes. Put gelatine in a small bowl with 2 tbs of water and dissolve over heat, mix with the treacle mixture. Whip cream until same consistency as treacle mixture and then fold ¾ of it into the treacle (keep the remaining ¼ for decoration). Whisk the egg whites until they hold their shape and fold in well with treacle mixture – leave until set. Add the remaining cream and sprinkle with nuts.

Serve with cream.

"A place for everything and everything in its place."

Mrs Beeton

Melting Moments

These very light little cakes of Scottish origin are now firmly established in Ireland, and live up to their name.

10oz (280g) butter

2oz (60g) icing sugar

8oz (225g) sifted flour

2oz (60g) cornflour

Lemon curd or thick honey

Cream the butter and sugar until very light. Add both flours gradually, mixing well. Put small spoonfuls onto greased baking trays and bake for about 12 minutes in a 180°C, 350°F, Mark 4 oven. Leave to cool on baking tray for 5 minutes, then remove and put onto cooling rack. When cold, sandwich together with a little lemon curd or thick honey in between. Makes about 30 'sandwiches'.

"The pleasures of the table belong to all ages, to all conditions, to all countries and to all eras."
Mrs Beeton

Ginger Shah Biscuits

If you try one of these biscuits, you'll want to eat the whole lot!

6oz (170g) margarine

6oz (170g) sugar

8oz (225g) flour

1 tsp baking soda

$^1/_2$ tsp syrup

2 tsp ground ginger

1 tsp cinnamon

1 egg yolk (optional)

Cream margarine and sugar together, add syrup and egg yolk.

Sieve dry ingredients together and fold into the creamed mixture, mix until a soft dough.

Roll into little balls the size of a walnut. Place onto baking sheet and press centre to flatten slightly.

Bake in a moderate oven until golden brown.

"A woman's place is in the home."

Mrs Beeton

Irish Flakemeal Biscuits (Oatcakes)

These biscuits can be eaten plain or as an accompaniment to any cheese.

4oz (115g) margarine

2oz (60g) sugar

2oz (60g) flour

$^1/_2$ tsp of salt

5oz (140g) flakemeal (porridge oats)

Pinch bicarbonate of soda

Mix all ingredients in a food processor.

Roll out and cut biscuits into required shapes.

Bake at 350-375°F/175-190°C for approximately 20 minutes.

Sprinkle with sugar.

"Tell me what kind of food you eat, and I will tell you what kind of man you are."

Mrs Beeton

Mulled Wine

To 3 bottles of red wine add

$^1/_2$ carton pineapple juice

$^1/_2$ carton orange juice

3-4 cinnamon sticks

1 cup (or more) sugar

1 orange pierced with cloves (4 or 5)

Orange & lemon slices

Apple – sliced

(add a spiced mulled wine 'bouquet'
sachet – optional)

Mix the ingredients together and serve from a bowl or big jug with ladle.

"Fizz" goes straight into the bloodstream. More than one glass of Champagne will put all of us over the drink/drive limit.

The Author's Tip On 'How To Cook A Husband'!

First, catch him when he is young. Select him yourself as tastes differ. Do not be misled by a silvery appearance, as though buying a fish. Do not go to the market as the best are always brought to your door. Be patient in the cooking of him or you had better go without. A good preserving pan of love is necessary. See that you wrap him in nicely washed linen, with tapes and buttons sewn on firmly. Tie him with a silken cord called comfort. (The one called duty is apt to be weak). Watch him carefully or he may get crusty at the edges. Keep a good fire of love, cheerfulness and put him near to it as suits him. If he fizzes and splutters do not be too anxious, some husbands do this until they are quite done. Add a little sugar in the form confectioners call kisses. (No vinegar or pepper on any account). If treated thus, you will find him digestible and agreeable, and he will keep as long as required unless put into too cool a place.

Recipe for Life

This was found amongst Patsie's personal papers after her death on 25th May 1996 and headed —

To Lara — with love

I hope I may have other grandchildren but, you, Lara, are my beloved first born grand-daughter and it is for you I am writing this. One day when you have a daughter of your own you may like to read her these words.

It is difficult when you are so young to imagine that your parents and your grand-parents were young too. We suffered and enjoyed, learnt and experienced most of what you face now – growing up is never easy and when you are grown up life will become even more difficult. I believe you already have two priceless assets – which I hope you will always keep – good health and a happy disposition and also a questing spirit and a fearless open mind.

Everything is an adventure and I hope it always will be so, however long you live.

There is never enough time to do everything – to see everything – to learn everything – to go everywhere or to achieve everything. There is always more to experience and enjoy. New friendships to make and old ones to keep in repair – new books to read and old ones to re-read – new places to visit and more music to enjoy.

The more you learn, the more you will realise how little one tiny human spirit can know is a short life span. But don't ever waste time – by waste I mean too busy to sometimes stand and stare or stop and think. Those quiet moments can be the most rewarding and the most fruitful. There will be moments of course when everything is black – perhaps someone you love dearly may hurt or disappoint you and everything may seem too difficult or utterly pointless. Remember always that everything passes and nothing stays the same or gets better or worse and every day brings a new beginning and nothing, however awful, is ever completely without hope.

Savour the moments of sheer happiness like a precious jewel – they come unexpectedly and with an intoxicating thrill. It may happen when you are walking down the street and the sun shines strong and the sky is blue or in a smile of spontaneous delight when unexpectedly you meet a kindred spirit and your thoughts are in harmony. Or in the thrill of poetry or the sound of music, which can raise your spirits and strike a chord in your heart.

Try to be tolerant. This is not easy, but never be ashamed of being intolerant when you know something is bad or wrong or hurtful to others. Kindness is one of the most important things in life and can mean so much. Try never to hurt those you love. Love is never needing to say you are sorry, but you will often have to apologise. We all make mistakes, and sometimes terrible ones too, but try not to hurt anyone for the sake of your own selfishness.

Don't ever to afraid to trust your own instinct. Seek advice from those you admire and trust, of course. Sometimes it helps to clarify things in your own mind by discussing them over with others. But in the end you will take the advice you want to hear – and you feel is right.

Try always to think ahead and not backwards, but don't ever try to block out the past because that is part of you and has made you what you are. But try, oh try! to learn a little from it!

It is more stimulating and exciting to try many things a little rather than one thing to perfection. To some rare and gifted people with a particular genius and quality this may seem wanton or wrong, but to most ordinary mortals it makes for a more interesting life.

Do everything – see everything – go everywhere – meet everyone and accept every invitation or challenge unless there is a very valid reason not to! Big opportunities hinge often on tiny ones – "When the ball rolls your way, grab it." We so rarely get a second chance, but miraculously this does sometimes happen too! The unexpected is always there and this is what makes life so exciting. I hope your life will be an adventurous one – nothing should ever be boring unless you make it so.

I hope your grasp will never exceed your reach.

Patsie Fisher

We may live without poetry,
    music and art

        We may live without conscience
          and live without heart

                We may live without friends
                 and live without books

                         But civilized man
                           cannot live without

                           COOKS!

Acknowledgements

I would especially like to thank my good friends, Shan Newman, who has drawn and painted the colourful sketches of the familiar scenes of Northern Ireland so beautifully and who has helped me in innumerable ways. Also to Faith Sutters who has skilfully designed and illustrated the front cover.

My thanks to dear Mrs Bell, who has given so much time to resurrect our most popular family recipes and who, together with Toni Edwards, has lovingly re-tried the chosen few in true Mrs Beeton style!

To my sister, Mary Rose, and my husband and children, I greatly appreciated their support; and their own especially created recipes. Also their helpful advice which appears on the pages where there are no attributable quotes!

I am indebted to Judge Hubert Dunn, Barbara Garland and Stephanie Mackenzie-Hill for their help and encouragement, and to Susan Cobb and Debbie Robinson for their patience and typing.

I would also like to thank Lynn New, the authoress, for her inspiration; and Ian McCorquodale and Ib Bellew for their guidance and time.

Finally, I acknowledge with great appreciation the tremendous influence of my serene and beautiful mother, Patsie. Her example of pride and enthusiasm for our family, both past and present, and the Women Caring Trust, which meant so much to her, gave me the confidence and interest to carry on her work.

To everyone who knew her – she made them feel special. So was she.

I dedicate this book to Patsie, with gratitude and everlasting love.